Mountains

Quinn M. Arnold

CREATIVE EDUCATION • CREATIVE PAPERBACKS

seedlings

000001845519940

Published by Creative Education and Creative Paperbacks
P.O. Box 227, Mankato, Minnesota 56002
Creative Education and Creative Paperbacks
are imprints of The Creative Company
www.thecreativecompany.us

Design by Ellen Huber; production by Joe Kahnke
Art direction by Rita Marshall
Printed in the United States of America

Photographs by Alamy (Kim Karpeles), Corbis (Stefen Chow/
Aurora Photos, Sumio Harada/Minden Pictures, Christopher
Kimmel/www.auroraphotos.com, Galen Rowell), Dreamstime
(Alexmak72427, Steve Byland, Cumypah, Espair, Aleksandr Frolov,
Hungchungchih, Isselee, Ian Kitney, Laurentiu Nica, Noracarol,
Jean-edouard Rozey, Andrei Stancu, Nantarpat Surasingthothong,
Chanon Tamtad, Tananddda, Testbild, Tassaphon Vongkittipong,
Xishuiyuan), iStockphoto (NaturesDisplay)

Copyright © 2017 Creative Education, Creative Paperbacks
International copyright reserved in all countries. No part of
this book may be reproduced in any form without written
permission from the publisher.

Library of Congress Cataloging-in-Publication Data
Arnold, Quinn M.
Mountains / Quinn M. Arnold.
p. cm. — (Seedlings)
Includes bibliographical references and index.
Summary: A kindergarten-level introduction to mountains,
covering their climate, plant and animal life, and such
defining features as their rocky peaks.
ISBN 978-1-60818-742-3 (hardcover)
ISBN 978-1-62832-338-2 (pbk)
ISBN 978-1-56660-777-3 (eBook)
1. Mountains—Juvenile literature.
GB512.A76 2016
551.43/2—dc23   2015041989
CCSS: RI.K.1, 2, 3, 4, 5, 6, 7;
RI.1.1, 2, 3, 4, 5, 6, 7; RF.K.1, 3; RF.1.1

First Edition HC 9 8 7 6 5 4 3 2 1
First Edition PBK 9 8 7 6 5 4 3 2 1

TABLE OF CONTENTS

Hello, mountain!

A mountain is a tall, rocky place.

Near the top it is cold and damp.

Bighorn sheep
jump from
rock to rock.

Mountain lions hunt up above.

Tall trees grow
at the base.
Woody plants
and wildflowers
are there, too.

It is cooler higher up the mountain.

Some peaks are snowy. The snow stays there all year.

Mount Everest is 29,029 feet tall. It is the tallest mountain on Earth.

People like to climb it.

15

Hawks fly between peaks.
Ground squirrels dig dens.

Pikas gather food
for winter.

Goodbye, mountain!

Picture a Mountain

peak

snow

cliffs

bighorn sheep

base

hawk

ridge

forest

21

Words to Know

base: the lowest part of a mountain

peaks: the highest parts of mountains

pikas: small animals related to rabbits

Read More

Hewitt, Sally. *Mountains.*
Mankato, Minn.: Amicus, 2011.

Riggs, Kate. *Mountains.*
Mankato, Minn.: Creative Paperbacks, 2016.

Websites

Easy Science for Kids: Tallest Mountains in the World
easyscienceforkids.com/all-about-the-tallest-mountains
-in-the-world/
Learn more about the tallest mountains on Earth.

PBS Kids: Mountain Scramble
pbskids.org/plumlanding/educators/context/mountain
_scramble.html
Play a game about mountain plants and animals.

Note: Every effort has been made to ensure that the websites listed above are suitable for children, that they have educational value, and that they contain no inappropriate material. However, because of the nature of the Internet, it is impossible to guarantee that these sites will remain active indefinitely or that their contents will not be altered.

Index